ANGKOR WAT

TRAVEL GUIDE 2024

Unveiling Angkor Wat: A Coastal Gem's,
Historic Wonders, Hidden Treasures and
Timeless Charms in 2024

Thomas A. Olvera

Table of Contents

1. INTRODUCTION

1.1 Overview of Angkor Wat

Nestled in the verdant Cambodian countryside, Angkor Wat is a testimony to the grandeur of ancient Khmer culture. This magnificent temple complex is widely regarded as the world's largest religious monument, covering around 162.6 hectares. Angkor Wat, a UNESCO World Heritage Site since 1992, is located in northern Cambodia, near the city of Siem Reap.

1.2 Brief Historical and Heritage Background

Angkor Wat dates back to the 12th century, during the reign of King Suryavarman II, and was built to honor the Hindu god Vishnu before becoming a

Buddhist shrine. The elaborate carvings on its walls portray events from Hindu epics such as the Mahabharata and Ramayana, demonstrating the centuries-long cultural blending.

1.3 Geographical Significance

Angkor Wat, located within the Angkor Archaeological Park, is surrounded by a huge network of temples and monuments, each representing a piece of Cambodia's historical puzzle. The park covers an area of 400 square kilometers and contains vestiges of the Khmer Empire, which once controlled Southeast Asia.

1.4 What makes Angkor Wat Unique?

Angkor Wat's architectural brilliance and symbolic significance make it a unique landmark in the world. The temple's five towers represent Mount Meru, the mythological home of the gods in Hindu-Buddhist mythology. The elaborate bas-reliefs tell stories about battles, cosmic events, and everyday life, demonstrating the Khmer Empire's artistic prowess. Angkor Wat is a one-of-a-kind and captivating location thanks to its combination of religious, historical, and artistic components.

1.5 Why Visit Angkor Wat in 2024?

While Angkor Wat has long been a popular tourist destination, the year 2024 has a unique fascination.

Ongoing restoration work and sustainable tourism initiatives have conserved and improved the site's beauty. This year's event offers a unique opportunity to see the temple complex in all of its glory, with increased accessibility and guest facilities.

The worldwide tourism scene is changing, and Angkor Wat remains a beacon of cultural diversity and historical relevance. Exploring Angkor Wat in 2024 allows tourists to immerse themselves in Cambodia's rich history while also witnessing the vibrant present. Furthermore, the year 2024 marks numerous major anniversaries relating to Angkor Wat's designation as a UNESCO World Heritage Site, making it an ideal opportunity for cultural lovers and history buffs to start on this enthralling journey.

In the parts that follow, we will delve deeper into the practical aspects of organizing a trip to Angkor Wat, seeing its historic glories, discovering hidden gems, and enjoying the ageless charms that make this place a true gem in the world of travel.

2. PLANNING YOUR TRIP

2.1 Best Time to Visit

Choosing the best time to visit Angkor Wat is essential for an unforgettable experience. The peak season, which runs from November to March, provides dry and warm weather, making it excellent for exploring the temple complex. However, during this time, more tourists visit, resulting in crowded attractions and higher rates. Alternatively, the off-peak season, which runs from May to October, offers lush scenery and fewer visitors, although expect occasional rain showers. Assessing personal preferences and weighing trade-offs will assist in determining the optimal moment to go on this cultural trip.

2.2 Entry Requirements

Before visiting Cambodia, travelers should be aware of the admission procedures. A valid passport with at least six months validity beyond the anticipated departure date is required. Most travelers are eligible for a visa upon arrival, which can be obtained at airports or border crossings. However, it is recommended that you examine the most recent visa laws and any changes to entrance requirements before departing.

2.3 Communication and Internet Access

While Khmer is the official language, English is commonly used in tourist areas. Learning a few simple Khmer phrases can improve your whole experience and establish connections with the locals. In terms of communication, obtaining a local SIM card upon arrival guarantees continuous connectivity. Major cities and tourist destinations provide good internet connectivity, which aids communication and navigation throughout the trip.

2.4 Budgeting and Costs

A realistic budget is necessary for a stress-free trip to Angkor Wat. Accommodation, meals, entry fees, and transportation must all be considered. While Cambodia is generally affordable, budgeting for guided tours, cultural events, and souvenirs enhance the experience. Researching and understanding the Cambodian Riel (KHR), as well as carrying a combination of cash and cards, allows you greater transaction flexibility.

2.5 How to Get There

Angkor Wat is primarily accessible through Siem Reap, the nearest city. Siem Reap International Airport (REP) accepts international aircraft, serving as the gateway to this historical site. Numerous airlines provide daily flights to Siem Reap from major hubs, allowing for easy travel. Taxis, tuk-tuks, and hotel shuttles are all available from the airport, giving you alternatives based on your tastes and budget.

2.6 Transportation Within

Getting around Angkor Archaeological Park demands careful transportation planning. Tuk-tuks, motorcycle taxis, bicycles, and rental automobiles are all available, catering to varied needs. Tuk-tuks are a popular and inexpensive option that provides a distinctive open-air experience. Guided tours provide vital insights, while bicycles enable unhurried exploration of the sprawling temple complex. Assessing individual comfort and preferences aids in selecting the most appropriate form of transportation.

2.7 What to Pack

Packing for a journey to Angkor Wat requires striking a balance between comfort, cultural sensitivity, and pragmatism. Lightweight and breathable clothing appropriate for tropical weather, comfortable walking shoes for exploring the temple complex, and a small daypack for carrying items for excursions are all must. Sunscreen, bug repellent, a refillable water bottle, and a cap are all vital for sun protection. To show respect, temple visitors should dress modestly, with shoulders and knees covered. A travel adapter, a first aid kit, and any necessary medications help to ensure a safe and happy journey.

In the following parts, we will delve into the historical wonders of Angkor Wat, explaining the significance of significant temples and unraveling the cultural fabric that distinguishes this UNESCO World Heritage Site.

3. ACCOMMODATION OPTIONS

3.1 Hotel and Resort

When organizing a trip to Angkor Wat, selecting the correct accommodations is critical for a comfortable and fulfilling experience. The area surrounding Siem Reap, the gateway to Angkor Wat, offers a broad choice of hotel alternatives to suit a variety of preferences and budgets.

Luxury hotels and resorts in Siem Reap provide exceptional comfort and services. Nestled in verdant environments, these institutions give a retreat-like atmosphere, with spa facilities, swimming pools, and fine dining restaurants.

Choosing a luxury resort not only ensures a relaxing getaway after a day of exploring but also adds a degree of indulgence to the overall experience.

3.2 Budget-Friendly Stays

Siem Reap features a plethora of guesthouses, hostels, and low-cost hotels for those on a tight budget. These hotels offer a pleasant and communal ambiance, encouraging friendships with other tourists. Many budget-friendly accommodations maintain a good level of cleanliness and provide basic facilities, ensuring a comfortable stay without breaking the bank.

Leaving the city center, travelers can find delightful guesthouses immersed in the local ambiance.

These hidden jewels frequently provide a more authentic experience, allowing visitors to connect with the community and get insight into Cambodian culture. Budget-conscious travelers should look into these options for a more immersive and culturally enriching stay.

3.3 Booking Tips

To make the most of your lodging selections, consider the following booking tips:

a. Early Booking Advantage: Booking rooms in advance allows you to secure preferred options and frequently at lower rates. Given Siem Reap's prominence as a tourist destination, particularly during peak seasons, early booking is recommended to receive the best discounts.

b. Read Reviews and Ratings: Before making a reservation, read reviews and ratings from other travelers on trusted websites. Platforms like TripAdvisor and Booking.com provide insights into the experiences of previous visitors, allowing you to make more educated selections about the quality and suitability of accommodations.

c. Consider Location: The location of your lodging is critical. While some may like the ease of staying in the city center, close to restaurants and stores, others may prefer a more remote location for peace. Consider the proximity to Angkor Wat and the various transit alternatives.

d. Explore Package Deals: Some travel firms and booking sites provide package deals that include lodging, tours, and transportation. These bundles can be both affordable and convenient, offering a comprehensive solution for stress-free travel.

e. Connect with Locals: Platforms such as Airbnb allow users to stay with local hosts, resulting in a more customized experience. Engaging with locals not only improves cultural immersion but also provides unique insights and recommendations.

f. Check Cancellation Policies: Given the uncertainty of travel, particularly in these times, it is prudent to review the cancellation policies of hotels. Flexible cancellation policies can provide peace of mind and flexibility in the event of unforeseen changes to travel arrangements.

In conclusion, Siem Reap's lodging options appeal to a wide range of interests and budgets. Whether you prefer the opulence of a five-star hotel, the camaraderie of a low-cost guesthouse, or the authenticity of a local homestay, the appropriate decision improves your entire experience of exploring the treasures of Angkor Wat. The next parts will dig into the historical wonders, hidden riches, and timeless charms that await visitors to the Angkor Archaeological Park.

4. HISTORIC WONDERS

4.1 Temple Layout

The Angkor Archaeological Park is a treasure trove of historical wonders, and comprehending the temple plan is essential for a rewarding journey. The park is separated into many clusters, the most renowned of which houses the beautiful Angkor Wat. Other important clusters are Angkor Thom, Ta Prohm, and Banteay Srei. Each cluster highlights distinct architectural styles and historical significance, providing a full journey through the Khmer Empire's heritage.

4.2 Angkor Wat Temple

The Khmer Empire's crown treasure, Angkor Wat, is a timeless architectural marvel. Its design depicts Mount Meru, the mythological home of the gods in Hindu-Buddhist mythology. The center tower, surrounded by four smaller towers, represents the peaks of Mount Meru, resulting in a harmonious and awe-inspiring construction. The exquisite bas-reliefs on the temple's walls tell epic stories from Hindu mythology, giving a visual feast for history buffs and art lovers.

4.3 Bayon Temple

Bayon Temple, part of the Angkor Thom complex, is well-known for its unique stone faces. The 54 towers have mysterious faces, which are thought to symbolize the bodhisattva Avalokiteshvara or a blend of King Jayavarman VII's visage and the bodhisattva. The temple's distinct combination of Hindu and Buddhist components symbolizes the empire's transition between the two religions. Exploring Bayon is a voyage through symbolism, complete with fascinating sculptures and interesting architecture.

4.4 Ta Prohm Temple

Ta Prohm, also known as the "Tomb Raider Temple," captivates visitors with its magical beauty. Ta Prohm, unlike the other temples in the park, has been kept mostly in its natural state, with giant trees and roots intertwining with ancient stones. The result is a hauntingly gorgeous sight that takes visitors to a bygone age. The temple's fame skyrocketed following its appearance in the film "Lara Croft: Tomb Raider," and it now stands as a testimony to the cohabitation of nature and human creativity.

4.5 Guided Tours

Exploring the historic wonders of Angkor Wat is made more enjoyable by taking a guided tour. Knowledgeable guides shed light on the cultural and historical significance of each temple, revealing the stories reflected in the carvings and architecture. Guided tours provide an organized itinerary that ensures guests see major landmarks while learning about Khmer history.

When deciding on a guided tour, consider the following:

a. A good guide can turn a visit into an educational and immersive experience. Look for guides who have studied history or archaeology and can provide detailed information.

b. Tour Duration: Because Angkor Wat is so large, excursions last different amounts of time. When deciding whether to go on a half-day or full-day tour, consider your tastes and physical capabilities. Full-day tours allow for more in-depth exploration but can be physically taxing.

c. Confirm if the tour includes visits to important sites including Angkor Wat, Bayon, and Ta Prohm. These sites provide a comprehensive overview of the Khmer Empire's architectural and cultural achievements.

d. Group Size: The size of the tour group can affect the overall experience. Smaller groups generally allow for more individualized encounters with the guide and a more in-depth investigation of the temples.

e. Transportation: Confirm that transportation is included in the tour. Some trips include air-conditioned vehicles, while others use tuk-tuks or bicycles. Choose a form of transportation that suits your needs and tastes.

Exploring Angkor Wat with a guide not only enriches historical understanding but also provides context for delicate details that may be missed on a self-guided tour. As we explore further into the hidden gems and outdoor experiences that surround Angkor Wat, the guided tour experience provides a firm basis for a thorough investigation of this extraordinary UNESCO World Heritage Site.

5. HIDDEN TREASURES

5.1 Lesser-known Temple

Beyond the well-trodden trails of Angkor Wat and its iconic equivalents, there is a realm of lesser-known temples that provide a more private and intimate encounter. Exploring these hidden gems allows visitors to see the intricate details of Khmer architecture without the masses. One such gem is Banteay Samré, a stunning temple in the Angkor Wat complex. Banteay Samré, with its well-preserved galleries and ornate carvings, exemplifies the Khmer Empire's creative flair.

Koh Ker, located in the northern half of the archeological park, is another example of Khmer innovation. Koh Ker, once the Khmer Empire's capital, is known for its towering prasats (temple towers) and tranquil ambiance. The voyage to these lesser-known temples reveals not only architectural marvels but also a peaceful atmosphere conducive to silent reflection amidst historical beauty.

5.2 Off-the-Beaten-Path Attractions

While Angkor Wat takes the focus, stepping off the usual route offers a tapestry of attractions that highlight Cambodia's unique cultural and natural history. Preah Vihear, built atop a cliff near the Thai-Cambodian border, has stunning vistas and a distinct architectural style from the Angkor temples. The route to Preah Vihear takes you through rural landscapes, giving you a glimpse into true Cambodian life.

The distant Beng Mealea, sometimes known as the "Indiana Jones Temple," offers an expedition through dense woods to access its extensive remains. This mostly unrestored temple allows visitors to imagine the grandeur of Angkor's temples before intensive preservation efforts. Exploring these off-the-beaten-path locations adds a sense of discovery to the voyage, providing a more intimate relationship with Cambodia's hidden gems.

5.3 Local Artisan Workshops

Beyond the stone-carved grandeur of Angkor Wat, Cambodia's rich artistic tradition is brought to life in local artisans' workshops. Siem Reap, the gateway to Angkor Wat, is a center of traditional craftsmanship. Visiting these workshops allows you to observe the development of exquisite handicrafts, textiles, and traditional Khmer art forms.

Artisans Angkor, a social company, exemplifies Cambodia's commitment to preserving traditional crafts. The workshop employs local craftspeople and provides training and fair pay. Visitors can explore the workshops and see the laborious process of making silk fabrics, stone carvings, and lacquerware. Purchasing handcrafted souvenirs directly benefits local artisans and helps to ensure the preservation of Cambodia's traditional heritage.

Engaging with local artists not only promotes greater respect for Khmer craftsmanship but also allows visitors to bring home unique and meaningful mementos. The workshops act as a link between the ancient glories of Angkor Wat and the colorful, living culture of modern Cambodia.

As we discover these hidden jewels, it becomes clear that Angkor Wat is more than just one sight; it is a portal to a plethora of experiences, each adding to the rich fabric of Cambodia's past and present. The tour via lesser-known temples, off-the-beaten-path sights, and local artisan workshops encourages visitors to dig into Cambodian culture and uncover layers of history that go far beyond the famed temples of Angkor Wat.

6. TIMELESS CHARMS

6.1 Sunset at Angkor Wat

Experiencing the sunset at Angkor Wat is a timeless tradition that captivates visitors with its ethereal beauty and the temple's reflection in the surrounding water. As the sun sets below the horizon, giving a warm glow to the old stones, Angkor Wat becomes a silhouette against the bright colors of the sky. The tranquil moat around the temple reflects the celestial spectacle, creating a mystical mood.

Choosing the best position to see the sunset is critical. The west side of the temple, across the reflecting pool, provides an unimpeded view of the sun setting behind Angkor Wat. As the day falls, the beautiful carvings on the temple's exterior are drenched in golden light, producing a captivating interplay of shadows and highlights. The serene ambiance of this twilight hour allows tourists to connect with Angkor Wat's spiritual and timeless allure.

While the sunset at Angkor Wat is a popular sight, it is best to arrive early to ensure an excellent viewing area. As the sun sets, the temple's shape blends into the multicolored sky, giving an indelible impression of Angkor Wat's ageless grandeur.

6.2 Sunrise on Bakheng Hill

For those looking for a different perspective, the sunrise at Bakheng Hill provides a wonderful and quiet experience. Bakheng, located near Angkor Wat, offers a panoramic view of both the surrounding environment and the famed temple itself. The journey to Bakheng Hill's summit is an experience in and of itself, frequently requiring a hike up a difficult trail or a trip in an elephant-drawn carriage.

Arriving at Bakheng before dawn allows visitors to see the gradual illumination of Angkor Wat as the first rays of sunshine break through the darkness. The temple's silhouette appears against the predawn sky, creating a mysterious and awe-inspiring spectacle. As the sky changes colors, from gentle pinks to blazing oranges, Angkor Wat's spiritual force becomes real.

The sunrise experience at Bakheng Hill is both a visual feast and a spiritual journey. The silence of the early morning, broken only by the rustling of leaves and distant sounds of nature, contributes to the meditative aspect of the moment. It is a time when the ancient stones of Angkor Wat appear to come alive, reverberating with the eternal spirit of millennia past.

Both daybreak at Bakheng Hill and dusk at Angkor Wat provide distinct vistas and atmospheres. Choosing between them may be determined by personal tastes, such as whether one prefers the tranquility of morning or the warm, reflecting glow of sunset. Regardless of the moment chosen, both encounters capture the eternal charms that have made Angkor Wat a pilgrimage place for people seeking a connection with history, nature, and Cambodia's enduring spirit.

As we embrace these ageless charms, we realize that the fascination of Angkor Wat goes beyond its historical and architectural significance. The interplay of light and shadow, reflections in the peaceful waters, and the serene moments of sunrise and sunset create a sense of timelessness that transcends the present, urging visitors to immerse themselves in the eternal beauty of this cultural treasure.

7. OUTDOOR ADVENTURES

7.1 Angkor Archaeological Park Trails

While the temples of Angkor Wat are the main attraction, the Angkor Archaeological Park provides outdoor enthusiasts with a network of trails that snake through the lush Cambodian countryside, providing a unique viewpoint on this historical wonder. These pathways not only provide a respite from the temple crowds but also lead to lesser-known structures and hidden gems inside the vast park.

a. Nature Trails: The Angkor Archaeological Park has nature trails that weave through lush jungles and reveal the region's abundant wildlife. These routes frequently lead to remote temples and old structures that are off the usual path. Walking along these routes allows tourists to observe the natural splendor that surrounds the historical sites, resulting in a beautiful blend of history and nature.

b. Countryside Cycling Routes: Cycling enthusiasts can explore the countryside around Angkor Wat on established routes. These trails lead riders through rural landscapes, attractive villages, and lesser-known shrines. Cycling allows for leisurely exploration and brings you closer to the local populations that flourish in the shadows of the old temples.

c. Historical Hiking Trails: For those looking for a more active adventure, historical hiking trails allow you to visit the temples by foot. These routes frequently feature ascents to elevated temples, which offer panoramic views of the surrounding environment. Hiking enables a more in-depth exploration of the temples' historical and architectural aspects while also enjoying the peace of nature.

d. Sunrise and Sunset Pathways: Special pathways have been developed for people who want to capture the perfect sunrise or sunset. These routes lead to strategic viewpoints with unimpeded views of the sun pouring its golden glow over Angkor Wat. The sunrise and sunset pathways are thoughtfully planned to provide a tranquil and meditative experience away from the hectic throng at the main temples.

7.2 Tonle Sap Lake Exploration

Beyond the temple-centric adventures, visiting Tonle Sap Lake offers an aquatic dimension to the outdoor activities around Angkor Wat. Tonle Sap, Southeast Asia's largest freshwater lake, is located just south of Siem Reap and provides a unique ecological and cultural experience.

a. Floating Villages: The lake is lined with floating villages, which include residences, schools, and markets erected on stilts. A boat tour of these settlements allows you to see how the locals live on a daily basis. The brilliant colors of floating dwellings and the bustling activities on the water provide a striking contrast to the ancient serenity of Angkor Wat.

b. Tonle Sap Lake is a sanctuary for birdwatchers and wildlife lovers. The lake's surrounding marshes and forests are home to a varied range of bird species, making it an ideal birdwatching location. Furthermore, the lake is home to a diverse fish population and maintains a thriving environment. Exploring the lake by boat allows for encounters with the unusual species that live in this enormous body of water.

c. Boat tours through flooded forests and floating gardens show how residents adapt to Tonle Sap's changing water levels. The floating gardens, which grow vegetables and fruits, demonstrate the lakeside community's creativity. Navigating across the small rivers amidst the rich flora offers a calm and immersive experience with the lake's natural beauty.

d. Cultural Immersion: Interacting with residents on Tonle Sap Lake provides a cultural immersion opportunity. Visiting floating markets, watching traditional fishing techniques, and engaging in community activities all provide insight into the lake communities' robust and vibrant lifestyles. It's an opportunity to learn about the people's connections to the lake and its natural riches.

Outdoor adventurers who explore the trails of the Angkor Archaeological Park and the waters of Tonle Sap Lake discover a lively and diversified Cambodia beyond the stone walls of Angkor Wat. These outdoor experiences combine the natural and cultural components that define the region, providing a more complete picture of Cambodia's past and present. Whether hiking through historical paths or drifting through floating towns, each trip adds a new chapter to the enthralling story of this Southeast Asian treasure.

8. CULTURAL EXPERIENCES

8.1 Traditional Performances

Immersing oneself in Cambodia's cultural tapestry entails attending traditional performances that highlight the country's artistic legacy. Siem Reap, the gateway to Angkor Wat, is a cultural hotspot, with traditional performances playing an important part in transmitting Cambodian stories and traditions.

a. Apsara dance is a traditional Khmer dance genre that developed in the royal courts of ancient Cambodia. Performers dressed in ornate costumes and wearing traditional jewelry tell stories from Khmer mythology with beautiful and symbolic motions. Apsara dance not only entertains but also represents Cambodia's rich heritage, showcasing the grace and refinement of Khmer arts.

b. Shadow Puppetry: Shadow puppetry, or "Sbek Thom," is a traditional Cambodian art form that mixes storytelling with exquisite leather puppets. A light source behind the puppets creates shadows on a screen, resulting in a captivating visual narrative. These performances frequently depict old myths and historical narratives, offering a distinct and entertaining way to interact with Cambodia's cultural history.

c. Live performances feature traditional Cambodian music, which is distinguished by distinctive instruments such as the Khim and Tro Khmer. These performances provide a melodious tour through Cambodian musical traditions, frequently accompanied by traditional dance. Attending a traditional music performance gives you a sensory immersion into the sounds that have echoed across the country for ages.

8.2 Festivals and Events in 2024

Exploring Cambodia in 2024 provides opportunities to engage in exciting festivals and events that reflect the country's cultural variety. Each festival is a mix of colors, music, and customs that offer a unique glimpse into Cambodia's modern cultural scene.

a. Khmer New Year (Choul Chnam Thmey): Celebrated in April, Khmer New Year is a festive celebration with water festivals, traditional games, and religious activities. Locals splash water to signify cleanliness and rejuvenation. Participating in Khmer New Year events allows tourists to experience the energy and camaraderie that distinguish this traditional holiday.

b. The Water Festival (Bon Om Touk) is held in November to mark the reversal of the Tonle Sap River's flow. This event features boat races, lit processions, and loud street celebrations. The Water Festival creates a lively and celebratory atmosphere in which communities come together to celebrate the spirit of unity and thankfulness.

c. Pchum Ben (Ancestor's Day) is a Buddhist celebration celebrated in September or October to honor ancestors. Families come together to make offerings at pagodas, and monks perform special rites. Pchum Ben invites tourists to experience the spiritual and familial components of Cambodian culture.

8.3 Local cuisine

No exploration of Cambodia's cultural riches is complete without sampling its unique and tasty food. Khmer cuisine reflects the country's history and location, merging influences from adjacent nations to create a delicious variety of meals.

a. Amok is a traditional Khmer dish made with fish or beef marinated in a thick coconut curry and cooked in banana leaves. The fragrant combination of lemongrass, galangal, and kaffir lime leaves adds a unique flavor to this culinary masterpiece. Amok is a must-try for those looking for a true flavor of Cambodian food.

b. Bai Sach Chrouk is a traditional breakfast meal made of grilled pork served over broken rice with pickled veggies. The dish's simplicity hides its savory impact, making it popular with both residents and visitors.

c. Num Banh Chok, often known as Cambodian noodles, is a breakfast staple. The rice noodles are topped with a green fish curry and a variety of fresh herbs and veggies. Num Banh Chok offers a delightful glimpse into the variety of Cambodian cuisines.

d. Fish Amok: This is another variant of the typical amok, with fish filets in a savory coconut stew. The meal is frequently cooked under banana leaves, which infuses the fish with a delicate blend of aromatic spices. Fish Amok showcases the culinary expertise that distinguishes Khmer cuisine.

e. Khmer Street Food: Discovering the local street food scene is an adventure in itself. The streets of Siem Reap provide a sensory voyage through Cambodia's gastronomic scene, with savory delicacies like Khmer spring rolls and sweet sweets like sticky rice with mango. Engaging with street sellers and sampling their offerings creates a real and engaging culinary experience.

Travelers become vital participants in Cambodia's cultural story as they attend traditional performances, celebrate holidays, and experience the pleasures of local cuisine. These cultural encounters enrich the tour of Angkor Wat, changing it from a historical landmark to a living, breathing tribute to Cambodia's lasting legacy.

9. TRAVELING BEYOND ANGKOR WAT

9.1 Nearby Attractions

While Angkor Wat is the crown gem of Cambodia's ancient wonders, the surrounding area is filled with additional sights that entice visitors to explore further. Beyond Angkor Wat, visitors can explore varied landscapes, immerse themselves in local culture, and experience Cambodia's present pulse.

- Angkor Thom: Angkor Thom, which means "Great City," is a sprawling complex that contains prominent structures including Bayon Temple, the Terrace of the Elephants, and the Terrace of the

Leper King. Bayon's enigmatic stone faces captivate visitors, while the wide terraces display elaborate carvings and historical significance. Exploring Angkor Thom is a continuation of the Angkor Wat tour, providing more insights into the Khmer Empire's magnificence.

- Banteay Srei, also known as the "Citadel of Women," is a modest but elaborately carved temple devoted to the Hindu god Shiva. The pink sandstone used in its construction enables intricate carvings that are very well maintained. Visiting Banteay Srei provides a contrast to the huge temples of Angkor Wat, highlighting the delicate beauty of Khmer architecture on a smaller scale.

- Phnom Kulen National Park: This sacred mountain range is a short drive from Siem Reap and provides a natural respite. The park is noted for its waterfalls, ancient temple ruins, and the iconic "River of a Thousand Lingas." Exploring Phnom Kulen provides a refreshing natural getaway as well as an insight into Cambodia's spiritual and historical dimensions.

- Floating towns: The neighboring Tonle Sap Lake is home to floating towns, where people live in stilted dwellings. Taking a boat excursion to these villages allows visitors to experience the inhabitants' daily routines, learn about their distinctive way of life, and appreciate Cambodians' connection to the water.

9.2 Day Trips

- Battambang: Battambang, a lovely town about a three-hour drive from Siem Reap, provides a slower pace and insight into Cambodian rural life. The town is famous for its well-preserved French colonial architecture, the Bamboo Train, and the Killing Caves of Phnom Sampeau. A day excursion to Battambang gives a refreshing break from Siem Reap's hectic pace.

- Koh Ker: Koh Ker, located about 120 kilometers northeast of Siem Reap, was originally the capital of the Khmer Empire. The location includes towering temples and monuments surrounded by lush flora. A day excursion to Koh Ker allows visitors to marvel at the ancient remnants while also learning about the Khmer Empire's historical legacy.

- Kampong Phluk: Kampong Phluk is one of the floating villages near Siem Reap, situated on the northern shore of Tonle Sap Lake. Day visits to Kampong Phluk provide a unique opportunity to navigate through stilted buildings, flooded woodlands, and the ebb and flow of life on the lake. It is an opportunity to experience the resiliency of communities that live in harmony with the changing water levels.

- Kbal Spean, also known as the "River of a Thousand Lingas," is a religious place in Phnom Kulen National Park. The riverbed has complex sculptures of Hindu deities and lingas, which are thought to purify the water as it travels downstream. A day trip to Kbal Spean combines cultural exploration with a hike through the lush woodland to uncover buried ancient treasures.

Beyond the stone walls of Angkor Wat, Cambodia emerges as a diverse location with a plethora of activities awaiting discovery. Whether touring neighboring landmarks such as Angkor Thom and Banteay Srei, taking day trips to Battambang or Koh Ker, or visiting floating villages and sacred rivers, each excursion contributes to a better understanding of Cambodia's history, culture, and natural beauty. Traveling beyond Angkor Wat provides new viewpoints and reveals elements of Cambodia's past and present that have yet to be explored.

10. PRACTICAL

INFORMATION

Traveling to Angkor Wat entails more than just admiring ancient monuments; it also necessitates practical preparations to ensure a pleasant and enriching experience. This thorough guide seeks to provide travelers with essential information for their visit, including health and safety guidelines and how to engage with locals.

10.1 Health and Safety Tips

a. Vaccination and Health Precautions: Before traveling to Cambodia, make sure you are up to date on normal vaccines and consider additional ones such as Hepatitis A and B, Typhoid, and

Japanese Encephalitis. Malaria prophylaxis may be recommended, particularly if you intend to visit rural areas.

b. Hydration and Sun Protection: Cambodia's tropical climate may be hot, so staying hydrated is essential. Bring a reusable water bottle and consume plenty of fluids. In addition, to protect yourself from the sun, wear sunscreen, a hat, and lightweight, breathable clothing.

c. Mosquito Protection: Dengue fever and other mosquito-borne illnesses are a major problem in Cambodia. Use insect repellent, particularly around dawn and dusk, when mosquitoes are most active. Consider wearing long sleeves and pants to provide additional protection.

d. Local Water and Food Safety: To avoid waterborne infections, use bottled or filtered water. To limit the danger of foodborne illness, consider street vendors with clean and hygienic settings.

e. Travel Insurance: It is recommended to have comprehensive travel insurance that covers medical emergencies, trip cancellations, and lost or stolen items. Check to see if your insurance carrier covers activities such as temple exploration and outdoor adventures.

f. Emergency Medical Facilities: Locate medical facilities in Siem Reap. SOS International Clinic and Royal Angkor International Hospital are reputed medical institutions that serve international guests.

10.2 Emergency Contacts

a. Emergency services:

Police: 117

Medical Emergency: 119

Fire: 118

b. Embassy Contacts:

- Embassy of your nation in Cambodia.

- Emergency contact details for your embassy or consulate.

10.3 Currency Exchange and Payment Methods

a. The official currency is the Cambodian Riel (KHR). While US dollars are generally accepted, it is recommended to carry some Riel for small purchases.

b. Currency Exchange: For competitive rates, exchange your currency at authorized money changers or banks in Siem Reap. Avoid exchanging money with illegal sellers.

c. ATMs and Credit Cards: Siem Reap has ATMs, making it easy to withdraw cash. Most hotels, restaurants, and larger shops take credit cards; however, smaller enterprises may prefer cash.

10.4 Connecting with Locals

a. Cultural Sensitivity: Show respect for local customs and traditions. Cambodians are typically friendly, although it is important to be aware of cultural differences. Dress modestly, particularly when visiting religious sites.

b. Learn Basic Phrases: While many Cambodians in tourist regions know English, learning a few basic Khmer phrases will help you engage more effectively and demonstrate respect for the native language.

c. Support Local Companies: Choose locally owned companies, including hotels, restaurants, and souvenir shops. This ensures that your travel expenses go directly to the local economy.

d. Participate in Responsible Tourism: Take part in activities that encourage responsible tourism, such as ethical animal encounters and community-based tourism projects. Be mindful of your environmental influence and work to leave a positive footprint.

10.5 Responsible Tourism Practices

a. Respect Cultural Heritage: Follow the guidelines at archeological sites and temples. Do not touch carvings or climb on buildings. Follow specified walkways and respect prohibited areas.

b. Reduce Single-Use Plastics: Cambodia has environmental issues due to plastic waste. Bring a reusable water bottle and think about adopting a refillable water purifying system to reduce single-use plastic use.

c. Wildlife Conservation: Use caution when engaging with wildlife. Avoid actions that use animals as entertainment. Support sanctuaries and conservation activities that promote ethical wildlife practices.

d. Minimize environmental impact by staying on approved trails, disposing of waste ethically, and using eco-friendly transportation whenever available. Leave natural and cultural sites just as you found them.

10.6 Useful Websites and Apps

a. Travel Advisory Websites:

- [Smart Traveler Enrollment Programme (STEP)](https://step.state.gov/).

- [World Health Organization (WHO): International Travel and Health](https://www.who.int/ith/en/)

b. Navigation Applications:

- Google Maps (https://www.google.com/maps)

- [Maps. me](https://maps.me/)

c. Language Applications:

- Duolingo (https://www.duolingo.com/)

[Google Translate](https://translate.google.com/)

d. Weather Applications:
- AccuWeather (https://www.accuweather.com/)

- Weather.com (https://weather.com/)

10.7 Local Customs and Etiquette

a. Greeting Customs: A small bow and a "sompiah" (pressing the hands together in a prayer-like motion) are customary Cambodian greetings.

b. When entering someone's home or a place of worship, it is traditional to take off your shoes.

c. Respecting Elders: Use both hands to give or receive something from an elder.

d. Monuments and temples: When visiting religious sites, dress modestly. Women should cover their shoulders, and men should not wear sleeveless shirts.

10.8 Language Tips and Useful Phrases

a. Basic Phrases:

Hello: "Sua s'dei"

Thank you: "Orkun"

Yes: "Chah"

No: "Te"

Excuse me: "Som tuk"

Goodbye: "Lea heuy"

b. knowing Khmer Script: While not required, knowing the Khmer script can offer a new level to your interactions. Online tools and language apps might help you familiarize yourself with the script.

As you embark on your vacation to Angkor Wat, adding these practical recommendations to your travel plans will improve your overall trip. From health and safety concerns to connecting with locals and adopting ethical tourism practices, these tips pave the way for an unforgettable and culturally enlightening journey. May your visit to Angkor Wat be more than just a tour of ancient ruins, but a meaningful journey into the heart of Cambodian history and culture. Safe travels!

11. NEW UPDATE AND EXPECTATIONS FOR 2024

As you plan your visit to Angkor Wat in 2024, stay up to date on the latest upgrades, changes, and expectations to ensure a smooth and enriching experience. From infrastructural improvements to rising trends, this guide will offer you vital information about what to expect on your journey.

11.1 Infrastructure Improvements

a. Transportation Improvements: Ongoing initiatives to upgrade transportation infrastructure are intended to give visitors more convenient travel options. Upgrades to the roads leading to Angkor

Wat, as well as the increase in public transportation services, help to make trips go more smoothly.

b. Visitor Facilities: Expect better restrooms, rest spaces, and information centers. These modifications are intended to improve the overall comfort and convenience of visitors to the Angkor Archaeological Park.

c. Expect technological integration to enhance the interactive experience. Audio guides, augmented reality apps, and technology-enabled signs will most likely be accessible to provide deeper insights into the temples' historical significance.

d. Sustainability Initiatives: Infrastructure upgrades may incorporate sustainable efforts such as waste management systems and environmentally friendly activities. Cambodia encourages responsible tourism, therefore these initiatives help to preserve the archaeological site and its surroundings.

11.2 Trends and Changes

a. Visitor Management: Expect to see changing visitor management tactics that strike a balance between site preservation and tourism. To manage the growing number of tourists, timed admission tickets, crowd control measures, and sustainable tourism practices may be put in place.

b. Cultural Experiences: Keep an eye out for specially planned cultural experiences and activities that will help you learn more about Cambodia's legacy. Cultural performances, workshops, and interactive activities can be created to provide visitors with a more immersive and instructive experience.

c. Digitalization of Services: As digitalization increases, more services will become available online. This includes ordering tickets, scheduling guided tours, and accessing informational materials via official websites and applications.

d. Preservation Initiatives: An increased emphasis on preservation initiatives may result in periodic closures or restricted access to specific places for restoration purposes. Stay up to date on any temporary closure notifications so you can plan your visit properly.

11.3 Frequently Asked Questions

a. Q: Do I need to buy tickets in advance?

A: While tickets can be purchased on-site, it is recommended that you obtain them ahead of time, especially during high seasons. Online platforms and official ticket booths in Siem Reap provide simple options for purchasing advance tickets.

b. Q: Are there any restrictions on photography?

A: Photography is generally permitted at Angkor Wat, though unique limitations may apply at various temples. Respect any signs stating limits, and be kind to other guests. Drones are usually not permitted.

c. Q: How Do I Avoid Crowds at Popular Sites?

A: Plan your visits intelligently, taking into account the time of day and the season. Early mornings and late evenings are frequently less crowded. Exploring lesser-known temples or taking guided excursions with off-the-beaten-path itineraries can also provide a more private experience.

d. Q: Is there a dress code when visiting temples?

A: There isn't a formal dress requirement, although it's best to dress modestly, especially while visiting religious sites. Both men and women should cover their shoulders, and knee-length shorts or skirts are preferred.

e. Q: Which currencies are accepted, and are credit cards widely accepted?

A: The Cambodian Riel (KHR) is the official currency, while US dollars are often accepted. Credit cards are often accepted at hotels, restaurants, and larger institutions, while cash is preferred for minor transactions.

f. Q: Are there guided tours available, and are they worthwhile?

A: Guided tours can enhance your experience by providing historical context and insight into the temples' significance. Knowledgeable guides may lead you through the complex, providing a better knowledge of the architecture and cultural significance of Angkor Wat.

g. Q: How can I help promote responsible tourism?

A: Select responsible tour operators and accommodations that value sustainability. Reduce your environmental effects by avoiding single-use plastics, adhering to local customs, and supporting local companies. Participate in community projects that benefit the local economy.

As you plan your trip to Angkor Wat in 2024, staying up to date on infrastructural changes, emerging trends, and practical concerns is essential for a memorable trip. The improvements are intended to improve tourist comfort, encourage sustainable tourism, and protect the cultural and historical relevance of Angkor Wat. By embracing these changes and practicing responsible tourism, you may embark on an unforgettable experience that not only uncovers historical beauties but also helps to preserve and appreciate Cambodia's rich legacy. Safe travels!

12. CONCLUSION

12.1 Summary of Angkor Wat's Allure

Angkor Wat, a cultural gem that stands the test of time, is located in the heart of Cambodia. As we wrap up our exploration, it's important to recap the fascination that has drawn visitors from all over the world to this enthralling place. Angkor Wat represents the Khmer Empire's architectural excellence and spiritual depth. Its elaborate carvings, soaring spires, and old courtyards tell stories from another period, enabling visitors to interact with the rich history inscribed into the stones.

The appeal of Angkor Wat goes beyond its historical significance. It is found in the interplay of light and shadow over its majestic structures, the peaceful reflection in the surrounding lakes, and the ageless beauty that captivates both the curious traveler and the seasoned historian. The temple complex's delicate blend of Hindu and Buddhist features produces a hallowed setting that exudes spiritual energy and invites study and thought.

The allure extends to the surrounding surroundings, which range from deep jungles concealing hidden temples to the tranquil waters of Tonle Sap Lake, where floating towns reflect the rhythm of daily life. It may be found at Siem Reap's vivid markets, where the colors, sounds, and fragrances form a sensory tapestry that immerses tourists in Cambodian culture.

12.2 Inspiring Future Travels

Reflecting on the wonders of Angkor Wat serves as a source of inspiration for future travels. Beyond the stones and carvings, it inspires us to explore other sites that combine history, culture, and natural beauty. It invites us to travel to lesser-known corners of the planet, where ancient tales are spoken through the winds and landscapes hide secrets waiting to be discovered.

The ethos of responsible tourism embodied by Angkor Wat encourages us to travel mindfully – to engage with local communities, respect cultural heritage, and positively contribute to the destinations we visit. It motivates us to be environmental stewards, reducing our impact on fragile ecosystems and supporting efforts that protect our planet's wonders.

Angkor Wat is more than just a destination; it's a journey through time, revealing layers of history and cultural depth. It serves as a reminder that travel is more than just visiting sites; it is also about connecting with a place's soul, comprehending its tales, and leaving a positive legacy.

In the spirit of Angkor Wat's attraction, let future journeys be motivated by a desire for meaningful experiences, cultural interaction, and a dedication to the sustainable and responsible exploration of our planet. As we carry the echoes of old civilizations and the beauty of varied landscapes in our hearts, let each voyage serve as an homage to the ageless appeal of discovery and the enduring spirit of wanderlust.

Printed in Great Britain
by Amazon

43910360R00050